LEFT GLOVE

Also by Mac Wellman

PLAYS

The Bad Infinity
The Land Beyond the Forest: Dracula and Swoop
Cellophane: Plays
Crowtet 1: A Murder of Crows and The Hyacinth Macaw
Crowtet 2: Second-Hand Smoke and The Lesser Magoo
The Difficulty of Crossing a Field
Two September

FICTION

The Fortuneteller: A Jest
Annie Salem
Q's Q
A Chronicle of the Madness of Small Worlds

POETRY

Satires
A Shelf in Woop's Clothing
Miniature
Strange Elegies

LEFT GLOVE

Mac Wellman

SOLID OBJECTS
NEW YORK

Printed in Canada

Design by Erik Rieselbach

ISBN-13: 978-0-9844142-0-8
ISBN-10: 0-9844142-0-7

Library of Congress Control Number: 2010933951

Special thanks to the MacDowell Colony. —M.W.

SOLID OBJECTS
P. O. Box 296
New York, NY 10113

LEFT GLOVE

A chorus of gloves enacts the Ballad of the lost LEFT GLOVE:

Quiet play as a Lemurian walkthrough.

YAMAHA NAZIMOVA, a glove loser
JEWEL BECKETT, a glove finder;

THE, the Indicator
AND, the Connector
IF, the Questioner
UM, the Thumb
ER, the finger farthest from Um;

MORPHO, Venus *Anadyomene*
in her nocturnal aspect as a
Luna moth;

Various other Moths and Spiders
(And, Er, Maths and other Myths);

and the CAHOON: A ghoul of affliction
and Hater of Lost Gloves.

CHORUS ONE

O morphology of error and error and Um.
O morphosis of our innocence that is a
now and The. Now and If. As it were
a noth noth nothing by way of thing but
did not care not as the addict his O
his O his morphine of Morpho dead to The.
Errrrrrrrrrrrrrrrrrrrr.

Dead to the world.

(And then some) says Um. Thus the
laying waste of time and error in this lost
glove loss loss lost. Lost lost lost. O ah
Er Um. Our I innocence undone by an
error in the in the glove department. Yes is
now become the doom stick. Death skulks
wickedwardwickedly all here and there his
central horn ablaze and his feet make
each stepping stone the track to a doom.
Loss of innocence our time has Morpho
suffered Morpho intensity of that rupture
and morphomomomottattattattattapalaka-
kaluza. Become a hollow moon place dead
to shame and the innocence of eyelashes. Shashes.
Shashes. Sashes. Shashes. Sashes. Shashes. Ah
pity thou the. The pity thy. The red bird's devil
delivery unto the state of Morpho genesis. A morphogenesis of
innocence splotched. Splotched
and splattered. (Splop)

Resolved, that: Yamaha Nazimova is accused by a CHORUS of gloves for the crime of losing her own (left) glove.

Resolved, a system of Whys and Choral somethings.

(Scene one.)

CHORUS 2

O hovering glove. O innocence of gloves.
Gloves of children. Gloves of squirrels.
Gloves of satin gloves of wood
gloves of cinnabar gloves of coal
gloves of turpentine gloves of brown ditch water
gloves of dispossession gloves of the elect.
Girl gloves and those of Captain Nonsense.
Gloves of the ether gloves of the wind
gloves locked in tiresome dispute gloves
pitch perfect in perfect consensus. Gloves
of the adored and adoring gloves
of the restless and bemused gloves
of the rapist and of the arsonist of the
safe cracker of the witless of the doomed.

All these gloves come and go all these
gloves are inscribed within a circle of chalk

White as the glove that hovers high above
O innocence of gloves O innocence of gloves.

A Narrow Way, Galleria or passageway between walls on two sides and perpendicular to two streets on the other two sides; an arcade; a thin place, known to some, unknown to many.

Traffic on foot, coming and going according to the clicks and whirs of Economic Calculus.

(Scene two.)

In a city somewhere, quite a large city perhaps and certainly a city quite pleased with herself.

CHORUS 4

O the sweeper does not sleep he sweeps he sweeps
And O the sweeper comes and sweeps and never
Sees and never sees and O the EVIL EVIL EVIL
Dust that is swept. And swupt and. Made to go away.
Doth not ever. Doth not ever. No it doth not.
O the sweeper does not because he doth not.
Sleep. Slupt and swupt. The fury of the sweeper

Answers not to sleep no she yes ah ah no she answers
Not to sleep but to sweep not to sleep but to
Sweep. Only sweep. The EVIL EVIL EVIL. Oh all the
Little things that are strewn about. All the little
Spider thoughts and bottle caps and toothpicks
And motes of dust and EVIL EVIL EVIL are not
No are not to be. Swupt totally. Because the sleep
Of the sweeper has too been swept away. SLUPT.
SWUPT. EVIL EVIL EVIL. O the eye of the sweeper.

O the sweeper does not sleep he sweeps he sweeps
And O the sweeper comes and sweeps and never
Sees what it is he sweeps and O the EVIL dust
That that. EVIL EVIL EVIL. Dust that swept. Dust
That grows invisible. Dust that dares not.
Dust that. Dust. Swupt and. Made to go away.
Doth not ever. Doth not ever. No it doth not.
O the sleeper does not because he doth not. Ever.
Sleep. But he doth not ever doth. Eye of the sweeper.
Also the eye of the sleeper doth not ever doth. No.
No no. See the glove there. See the glove there
Someone just left behind. No no no. Just left behind.

We see several dead gloves, none of them (g)lovely; none of them our glove.

The Right Glove has a bad thought, rejects the Left one O error O error:

Vivth CHOOOOORUS:

Resolved, that.
The Right Glove shall not know the Left
Glove, nor be a party to her doings; that
The Right Glove shall repair to her place
Of dwelling and not be O not be seen with
Nor have congress with the Left Glove in
All her doings, actions, fits, sudden excitations,
Flurries of twitching and grasping of all;
Nor shall the Left Glove be apprised of voyages
& pilgrimages of the Right Glove in far domains
Where Right-Handedness is the preferred and
Established mode of articulation, of the rule
Of manual performance (O Hands!) as she pertains
To gripping, grasping, holding, and unholy
Acts of screw to the right unscrew to the left,
Tweezers, scissors, applications of powders
And creams and related though distinct
Acts of combing and shaving, and axe
Wielding and hammering and holding
High the Libertarian Torch even in acts of
Rapine unjustifiable slaughter looting pillage
And desecration considered solely as acts
Of a manual nature of the O Tribe of Opposable
Thumb. Um. Thumb shall be honored in all such
Acts, even as dubious as painting, writing,
And twisting of wires and the troublesome act
Of unraveling of balls of string the Adversary
Hath so confused as to defy the cunning of the
Left and the rectitude of all that is Right.

(Silence. Pause. Silence.)

6th CHORUS

Wide is the way. Innocence. Nothing nothing more.
Wide is the way. Narrow is the passage to. Nothing
No no no no no no no. Not a thing in nothingness
Hath a tail like innocence. Wide is the way.
Innocence. Innocence indoors and out nothing
Nothing more nothing much nothing less than
Wide is the way. Narrow is the passage to. Nothing.
Is what fills the empty glove. Nothing is the hand
Of nothing. Nothing wears the glove you lost. Lost
No no no no no no no it is true you lost the glove.
Wide is the way. Innocence. Nothing nothing more.
Wide is the way. Narrow is the passage to. Nothing
No no no no no no no. Not a thing in nothingness
Hath a tail like innocence. Wide is the way.
Innocence. Innocence outdoors and in nothing
Nothing more nothing less than nothing much. O.
Wide is the way. Narrow is the passage to. Nothing
Is what fills the empty glove. Nothing is the hand
Of nothing. Nothing wears the glove you lost. Lost
In time. Lost in space. The error is yours.
The loss is yours the glove is no longer yours.
Innocent the glove. Innocent the glove.
Nothing wears the wear. Nothing shall wear the glove.
Till time topples all the towers of crime and error.
Till all gloves are reunited, both the Left and the Right.

Till all hath a tail like innocence.
Till all the gloves creep to their salvation.
Till what is lost is found. Left and Right.
Wide is the way. Innocence. Nothing nothing less.

(Scene three.)

A young woman, Yamaha Nazimova, accidentally drops her glove
on the
the left one
a
a, Er,
singleton
in the air,

plop,

on the ground. Her

done. 5 pm. Unknowing, she walks away (unseeing).

CHORUS 3

[The lost Glove says]
Perhaps there is a plug that fits in in the hole. Oh yes
there is that plug there must be there must be Oh
yes because that plug is of an innocence in the
highest degree like a white dove high in the O O O
yes in the highest branch of the highest tree lovely.
All the passageways lead to that hole. Plug it up.
All the galleries tilt in that direction. Plug it up.
What fits is what fits is is what fits that hole
and the rickety door has fallen from the hinge swark
and the granite stone has been split and swark is
broke and the way into the sea blocked blocked swark
with old newspapers and the cats swark of the night
hath a muscle that is red light white light and swark
light of a leprous condition Swark. Oh innocence Oh
innocence. All the plush red pin cushions have gone gone home.
Swark swark swark. Gone to home.
All the homes are filled with foam rubber and the
innocence of mice and rats and inflatable bullfrogs.
All the holes are waiting to be plugged up.
All the innocence of apples is lost to care.
All the apples are red as beets. Swark. And all
the beets are red as the radish and and
tomato even the innocence the innocence of
redvermillionattattatttattattatpalakakaluza.
Perhaps there is a plug that fits in the hole. Oh
redvermillionattattatttattattatpalakakaluza.

SEVENTH KOR

Resolved, that the person in question, one
Yamaha Nazimova, is alleged to have
Committed an Error, in infamy, in the
Losing of her left glove. Left glove left.
Yamaha Nazimova, a person of whom
Nothing is known. Not where she comes
From. Not where she goes. Not what she
Does if any doing she doth. Her said character
A mystery. Likewise the place of her birth,
Age, status, comportment, and deportment.
Nay . . .

Committed said act of misplacement
During one early morning on the 23rd
Day of the Month of — of the Year of
— at the hour of the Sorrow of the Left
Glove and the Glee of the Right. Yea . . .
For the rush of events is such that.
For this precipitate act stands as an. An act
Committed in Error and in infamy of lost
Glove, lost during a rush of events. An
Errand of an unspeakable kind. If so,
The character of a true crime. Yamaha:
Is she a piano tuner? Is she a piano?

And if softly why not loud? And if she is a
Nazi? And her motivation a Nazi motivation?
Dread. The dread that clouds the minds
Of all the other gloves in her possession.
Left ones in particular. For what if. What if
The Right Gloves have conspired in this crime?
What if? Yamaha Nazimova, a person of whom
The less said the better may she may she be sent far
Far away where she and her crime will be as a light
That is turned off and out. That is turned out and off.

(Scene four.)

Ungloved, walks rapidly from dot: a) to
dot: b)
at
opposite ends of the arcade, un
Um
unknowing.
An
Error, long rehearsed in time's glove, is released;
Error is released;
Ah yi ah yi ah yi …

…

KOR OCHO

Resolved, that the Left Glove
Cannot be half of the moon,
Nor be a green of cheese. For,
O, does not the forest fill up?
And, O, does not the glove of
The fox glove sharpen the? O,
And does not the forest fill up
And not go ghastly green till
Resolution cries out? Yes,
No it is not that of the Left
Nor of the Right that pricks
The ear that prickles the nape
And cannot be the Green Face
Of the Moon and Gem and Eye;
Resolved, that the Right Glove
Cannot be the other half of, of
What is green and not gladdest
Gold. Because the Way of the
Thing that is an, O, a pair of,
Of gloves does not have a,
A merest and only one end.
One end only, one end only.
Way follows a line from a)
And O does the glove of the
Foxglove not sharpen the? O,
And that line must end in b);
Both gloves, both Left and Right
Feel sharpness of the foxglove bite.

NINTH CHORUS~

RESOLVED, the somersault of the lost glove
be not forgotten, be not a blot and smear
upon the workings of what it is that works;
be not forgotten, be not become a nothing
to the whole damn boom diddy diddy boom;
boom diddy diddy diddy boom; BOOM BOOM.
THAT all lost gloves, whether Right or Left,
be recalled from their secret hiding places;
and be led to this place boom diddy diddy boom;
boom diddy diddy diddy boom; BOOM BOOM.
That all lost gloves, whether of the Right or
of the Left, be awakened from their slumbers,
from their dream of a better time, from the
nightmare of abandonment, of being lost;
THAT all lost gloves be assembled, here and now,
in the old city of Hand-Shoe, and wake as
from a dream that was like a thing of cloth
sheathing each of the five in a hat of cloth,
hat of leather, hat of fur, hat of beaten metal;
and be led to this place boom diddy diddy boom;
boom diddy diddy diddy boom; BOOM BOOM.
SO THAT justice may prevail; so that what
is lost may be recovered and restored; BOOM BOOM;
Boom diddy diddy diddy boom boom boom, [Pause]
boom diddy diddy diddy boom boom boom,
boom diddy diddy diddy boom boom boom.

CHORUS TEN: *Left Glove*

One Yamaha Nazimova:
Place of birth: unknown;
Country of origin: unknown;
Occupation: unknown;
Appearance: unknown;
Height and weight: unknown;
Languages spoken: unknown;
Deportment: unknown;
Emotional condition: unknown;
Intelligence Quotient: unknown;
Terms of employment: unknown;
Education: unknown; if applicable —
Terminal degree: unknown; if applicable —
University status: unknown; if applicable —
Sports and hobbies; unknown;
Ethnicity; unknown;
Age: unknown;
Friends and colleagues: unknown;
Size of glove: medium.

CHORUS ELEVEN

Resolved, that:
The glove that is named, named Left Glove,
be not forgotten, an image floating, as if
a mere blip or bleb in clear-air disturbance;
that the name of Left Glove be honored

in all the halls and malls the world over;
that the name of Left Glove circle the world
three times over, so rapid the telling of her
fame, her excellence, her cheerful countenance;
that the name of Left Glove be as a solemn
music to the deaf ears of the Right Glove clique;
that all good men shall hum that melody
without knowing what it is they hum nor why
nor will they care to know, being in harmony
with all that goes covered in a sheath —
whether it be of cloth or felt, or finest satin
with intricatest stitching or smoothest leather
of a buttery softness; Nay, rubber gloves of
the surgeon healing the wounded; nor the Latex
Glove of the Dentist focused, with sharpest
Eye on the bad Tooth; nor of a corresponding
roughness and robustness, winter gloves
of the world at the extreme Polar antipodes;
nor of the bear paw of the indigenous one, nor
the lion paw of the one who practices the arts
of Lion Craft where the big cats roam and
growl and glower, and fear not the Strong
Bow and Spear, but bow only to the White
Glove of the small person with flowing hair whose
glove signifies the Inwit of Excellence and the
excess of all that goes in glory wherever
what is sheathed in the excellence of gold and
silver, glows and goes. And grows and it glows.

(Scene five.)

A long and narrow covered area, narrow and open at both ends a

walkway and thin place less

than a room (who thinks up such places?),
A
a
An,
Er,
another.

Far far far to the exact spot where a

Planar field is as   as   a sidereal day and:
Error’s errand has completed her (one-gloved) stroll.
Um, Er.

Ground glove unmoving, lost abandoned, but hatching plots.

Dark leather plots governing the final disposition of things.
Dispersal. Of The. Of If. Of And. Of Um, Er.

Dark mattcr’s clsc.

Dark matter’s else disturbs the Left Glove with a   a   a oh bad mad dream:

CHORUS 12

Resolved, that:
Five big fat crows for fingers, five big
Flat black crows waddle in a sea of grass
Each one a finger a finger fled from a
Left Left Glove. Fingers out of joint out
Of hand, O, may they scurry may they scrabble
In a consternation of crows, flurry home
Five big fat crows for fingers, five big
Flat black crows waddle in a. Sea of grass
Each one a. Finger a finger. Fled from a
Left left. Glove fingers out of joint. Out
Of hand, O, may they. Scurry may they scrabble.
In a. Consternation of. Crows flurry. Home
Five big fat. Crows for. Fingers five big
Flat. Black crows waddle in. A sea of. Grass
Each one a. Finger a finger. Fled from. A
Left. Left Glove. Fingers. Out of. Joint out
Of hand, O. May they. Scurry may they. Scrabble
In. A. Consternation. Crow. Flurry. Home
Five. Big fat. Crows. For fingers five. Big
Flat. Black. Crows waddle. In a. Sea of. Grass
Each one. A. Finger a. Finger fled. From. A.
Left. Left Glove. Fingers out. Of joint. Out
Of hand. O. May they. Scurry. May they. Scrabble.
Five. Big fat. Crows. For. Fingers five. Big
Flat. Black Crows waddle. In a. Sea. Of. Grass.
Each one. A. Finger a. Finger. Fled. From. A,
Left. Left Glove. Fingers out. Of. Joint. Out
Of hand, O, may they scurry may they scrabble home.

The eye's range and extent and scope and field of
Er, Um,
a focal array:

(O Steersman (in the night sky) . . .

KOR THIRTEE(E)EEN~

Resolved, that
As night is the moon's glove; and
As day is the sun's glove; and
As all things far are as a glove
To all things near and as time
Is to space as a long and elegant
Glove of the evening so long so white
So cunningly sewn and fitted that
She will never hike up at the forearm
Nor will ever rumple at the wrist
Nor effect the error of itch and burn
The skin of the space of the world as
She tilts in time to the music of time
As the ungloved go sadly about at
Night like blind actors who bang
Against each other, collide
And go bump and go bump bump
Like the end of the world and all, O,

All she contains, stumbled against
And broken: Poor dumb thing.
Poor dumb thing, forever unable;
Poor dumb thing, forever unable
To set right what has been shattered;
To set right what has been mangled;
To set right what has been splintered;
To set right what has been riven
In twain by the uncouth and ungloved
Dumb thing who thinks a glove is not as night is to the
moon, O.

(Scene six.)

High above the ground. In the far distance one strange cloud too far too geometric for whose own his her own damn good; a simple scattering Watling Street of Monsoor Um and Er; Eye through the hole of: Oh.

A

Place far far. A
place no glove has quipped no glove hath
reached
for. What

is this quiet?

Lemurian walk-through. A something someplace someone few of A off of A. And all of them ungloved.

ℒ

CHORUS 14 *unfinished*

Resolved,
All Errand is not error YEA if she go gloved;
All Errand is comely, if she go gloved; all fruit
Ripens soft and glovely; and if she go gloved
All Mothery is of a powdery perfection, if she
    but go gloved;
All Spider persisteth in glorious WEB,
    if she but go gloved;
All Mathesis be of elegant perfection; if she
    but go gloved;
All Morpho be Venus, "born of the foamy sea"
    if she go gloved; for
All Errand is not error YEA if she go gloved;

But, NAY, for

All cahoonery be trampled underfoot;
          for she walks with no glove & spiteth
                    and spitteth upon the one who is lost;

Er, and then:

Finished CHORUS 14

Resolved,
All Errand is not error YEA if she go gloved;
All Errand is comely, if she go gloved; all fruit
Ripens soft and glovely; and if she go gloved
All Mothery is of a powdery perfection, if she
          but go gloved;
All Spider persisteth in glorious WEB,
          if she but go gloved;
All Mathesis be of elegant perfection; if she
          but go gloved;
All Morpho be Venus, "born of the foamy sea"
          if she go gloved; for
All Errand is not error YEA if she go gloved;

But, NAY, for

All cahoonery be trampled underfoot;
        for she walks with no glove & spiteth
                and spitteth upon the one who is lost;
All lostness of gloves is to be trampled underfoot;
        for she walks with no glove;
AND the glove that is lost is lost FOREVER;
And the glove that is lost is driven far far away;
And the glove that is lost must await,
        alone, in the empty arcade;
Must await the coming of Jewel Beckett;
        and must hope against hope;
Must despair of all hope if she pass, YEA,
        without seeing and must join all the other
Lost gloves, standing alone, at the end of time

(Scene seven.)

An errand on the stroll. Error's. Someone goes someone stays. The, And, If, Um, Er: all of A (un)gloved

unhoused and empty.

CORUS FUNFTEEN

Resolved, that
A certain Jewel Beckett be crowned with a
        glove of gold and silver silk;
May her name be a byword among all the
        tribes of glove, especially the ones
Lost in the world, hopeless, then found in a flash;
Lost to the many, who care not and proclaim:
WHAT is a lost and left glove to me, HA!
        For I am a man of finance, terrible in wrath;
What is a lost and left glove to me, HA!
        For I am a creature of Television, with many teeth;
What is a lost and left glove to me, HA!
        For I am a genius of rubber and salt;
For I am a person of Importance, beyond reproach;
For I am a professor of Ultimate Truth;
For I am concerned with the Immortal Soul,
        and not, HA! with the poor gloves of men;
For I am a lady not to be trifled with, HA!
        What is one glove to me without the other?
For I am a desperate person, upwardly mobile;
        and my mind is a ceaseless whirring of wheels;
For I am a student, HA! appalled by the books,
        (dull and incomprehensible) and am fearful of
                consequence;
For I am whoever I am, not like this person,
        this nobody, this person of no bearing,
        no consequence — average, nondescript, of no power and
        influence, this stranger, Jewel Beckett, who is said to be
        neither beautiful nor rich.

CHORUS SIXTEEN: *Left Glove*

Resolved:
that the Left Glove be not covered by the Right;
Resolved, that the Right Glove be not covered by
the Left; Resolved, that the might of gloves be worn
in day as in night; be resolved, that Sebastian
fall down in folly; be resolved, that the mighty find
woe past their glory; Resolved, that the ungloved
become a glove for the weak; resolved, that
the weak fear not the glove of the holy; resolved, that
gloves be as gloves & bask in the glove of even-handedness;
resolved, that all is as was shall be, and gloveliness and
gloveitude be forever in glove history:
Boom, diddy diddy diddy boom, boom, boom;
boom, diddy diddy diddy boom, boom, boom;
boom, diddy, diddy diddy boom, boom, boom;
May all the gloves be as one glove, except for the unhappy for the
        hands of the godly are covered with fingers more numerous
        than stalks of celery;
in the fields of Gethsemane, for the gloves of the lovely
        be as stars of the night; May the gloves of the angry yield to
        the gloves of the meek;
May the gloves of the hungry be filled with oats and hay;
May the gloves of the thirsty be filled with water and wine;
May all gloves speak as one glove, except when they are many;
May there be no division among gloves; May there be only consent
        among the many-fingered cloth that is the Glove of
        Consciousness, the Glove of Time, the Glove of Beginnings,
        Endings, and the glove beyond these that holds up the sky;

Boom, diddy diddy diddy boom, boom, boom;
boom, diddy diddy diddy boom, boom, boom;
boom, diddy, diddy diddy boom, boom, boom;

∽

An infinite gallery, an arcade, a thin place leading to a far far domain hath opened up on a a a

way less thin than by distance

a dot.

∽

CHORUS seventeen

Resolved, that:
We who know,
shall not know how;
shall not know how
to Inch and Foot;
shall not know end
from start and up
from where up goes
at the sheer drop
of an inch at rest.

Resolved, that:
We who know,
shall not know how;
shall not know how
to Inch and Foot;
shall not know end
from start and up
from where up goes
at the sheer drop
of an inch at rest.

This is the test that fingers five
obligate and make of it a
miracle: One two three four five.
What gloves the hand gloves the eye
and heart and soul and pins the
name of Inch to each as a mile's joy.
Resolve this; resolve that,
in the name of a Left Glove left behind.

KOOOOR 18

Resolved, that:
Glove may accomplish Inch, make the pin drop.
Glove may move, like a silence,
among the knowing
as a pin dropped;
as a show of dazzle upon the brow
of each one who hurries past;

as a shadow of the stick bug;
as a diametric Inch
measures the earth with no double;
as though she flew with no troubles.
As though she flew the coop, shrilling,
to measure the world, not her double;
as a diametric Inch;
of each one who hurries past;
as a show of dazzle upon the brow.
As a pin dropped
among the knowing
Glove may move, like a silence;
Glove may accomplish Inch, make the pin drop.
That resolved, resolve that.
O: Glove, Inch, pin, silence, show;
Dazzle, brow, shadow, bug, Inch;
Earth, double, Inch, shadow, bug;
each one shadows show and each brow
as a pin dropped
among the knowing.
Glove may move, like a silence,
Glove may accomplish Inch and call it Mile;
        that resolved, resolve that.

∽

Thought's glove heats up shot's tower looks up thinks up gravity looks down Oh and all things pertaining to the glove to the graveyard and goeth a) to the direction a) b);

(of those mad wood mad)

Arrow's (evil) direction an instant a

as a metropolis a polity not unlike this one. A hill not a city on a. Hill (hell).

A thing (t)here.

Planar field as on a sidereal day and.

Held in tight focus.

Held in wide focus.

∽

CHORUS NINETEEN

Resolved, that:
One glove among many, lost in an instant;
found the next; bow and then rise;
gloves in a chorus arrive and then go;
one after another, tap out time.
One glove among many: folded, flung;
lost in a moment, in eternity found.
A chorus of gloves; fingers in the fog,
one after another, tap out time.   One
after another, five fingers flared;

lost in the walkway, found near the moon;
a chorus of gloves, O whitest angels;
each upon each, hey! Perform the old taratantara;
one among many, twirls like the autumn
    leaf, alive in the vortex;
What do we know? Does anyone know?
Lost in the gallery, O, O, no one looks down;
gloves upon gloves trek across Asia,
    black with dust, spangled caravansary.
Each after each measures the odd Inch;
one glove among many,
fingers alert as pointed ears;
one glove among many,
one glove left, one glove left behind.
Nothing matters, nothing matters;
but for a lost glove the firmament
creaks and breaks asunder;
O bow and then rise; O bow and then rise;
    O bow and then rise!

CHORUS 20

Resolved, that:
One thing is connected to another, just as
one glove is part of a pair, irrefutable.
One thing is next to another, just as
the trees in the meadow are just where they are.
One glove is part of a pair, irrefutable;
and all pairs are to all other pairs of glove

as leaves are to branches and branches to trees;
as Inch deep in the wild wood
is type and portrait of
the Inch in paradise.
The Inch at City Square authenticates the Inch
on the dry valleys of Mars.
All things are as fingers of glove,
hover with joy over the task at hand.
Fingers are not idle in the mind.
Fingers are not idle in the dream.
Fingers delight in the Inch and Foot —
they measure and march and seek out
a synchronous pattern of coincident
movement impossible to describe;
impossible to inscribe in a circle
of chalk only a foot wide on the
        walk-way of the Narrow Place and arcade
        and Galleria and thin place because
there is HUSH a thin place HUSH a thin place
        of the world
connecting HUSH HUSH all twin gloves as though
they were hammered as one, and riveted thus.
Resolved this, thus.
Fingers are not idle when they go gloved;
fingers are delights in all things (g)lovely.
One glove left, one glove left behind.
Nothing matters, nothing matters;
but for a lost glove the firmament
creaks and breaks asunder;
O bow and then rise; O bow and then rise;
        O bow and then rise!

21 KOR

Resolved, that
Glove hath no conclusion, hath no
end point, neither in time nor in hand;
Glove hath no cataclysm, hath no
artifice of the digital, hand's diametric
needle & compass pin; Glove hath no
notion of the pointed, nor of pointless error.
A Glove has a soul like any puppet,
sure thing of desire, wooden eyes, wooden
hair, an oar floating among water reeds
as lovers drift by, indifferent to all else.
A Glove has a soul like any nightshirt
though you cannot see her shadow
because the soul has not a seething-veil
to undertake the dark night-walk, O,
eerie metacarpal taratantara O!
O! O! O many-fingered dance of gloves!
Glove has no mind to make up;
her conclusions are reached Inch
by Mile, both in time and in the hand;
Glove has no catastrophe; her patience
is drying paint to the flickering Moon,
lost in phases, like humankind, aglow
in night or on the summer haystack
as if no clock spoke, no hair grayed.
Glove will stay, quiet, where you drop her;
Glove does not bother if another one appear.
Yet Glove is not an adjunct to anything;
her face is bright, and she is always where she is;

she is always where she is. Where she is, she is there.

Resolved, The:

A such and such is about to, in the narrow place, by the long
shadow, is about to yes, maybe is a

;

and picks up A, daintily, as it were, between
Um and The

thumb and forefinger; Um, The (Jewel Beckett);

Resolved, that The:

She looks askance.

Poor Oh Er thing.

Noth it is nothing. Noth not. (Moth)

Nothing but the loss and care in. A.
The.

Choral somethings chitter — resolved, that:

Mystery be a space and an abyss. An.

Argument against.

Perpetuity.

Who one one is say the of she too to whom
So
Ever. It is it; it is it's
yit.

Yit yet yut. Perpuppytuity. Yit's

domain. Time scaled down to a level to a plain spot arcade Galleria
thin place open to a a open to the

A,
An, Er,
Um;

Goes in error, goes as A as a a line drawn in the

Resolved, that Yamaha Nazimova did do and did drop A and left it
right,

(Smack) there I am in a a a pointing sense moving as a dot
does,

X, the place where

ℐ

Cahoonery

[*Cahoon:*
ghoul of lost
glovedness

ℐ

The, the Indicator
And, the Connector
If, the asker of questionummumms. All

pointed, thus, here at there:

Her. (His)

ℐ

A filched glove?

7 pm the black glove bays as a shadow shadows A.

Only where my fingers missed are now and and hold nix and all five and branchiate nothings at A.

8 and 9 and 10 pm.

No; no; no; no; noth um hung (hing);

ask The not for And and If are Um tipped off by Er:
Go: To empty places and testify that, to

(Resolved, that)

Testify to a a a ghost way far down light's pinhole, endlessness of an infinite regress there in a far afar domain a a a beyond city and plain;

Er; Um;

a morphology not of ours, gloved in an

alien

narrow way and thin place The And If Um Er,

infinite, as it

was and is too, dear lost glove.

Time's wand O.

Dark missing glove says her prayers as night.

Night with hooks and teeth.

At midnight Morpho appears:

We must leave this world.

. . .

Morpho interrogates A as all spaces, as spaces (only where?)

Follow them out the out way them as the tip of The.

Outs.

Resolved, that:

(22nd CHORUS:

Resolved, that:
Right Glove too shall fall down in folly,
for what is Right without Left, Up
without Down, Sun without Moon?
Right Glove too shall dread
a night when useless she
shall be flung, flung far away,
far from care and home and hearth,
but in full consciousness, O,

the coming disaster, just at brink.
Right Glove too shall fall down in folly:
shall hear the verdict spoken in dead calm;
shall be led to the place & be tied, tied
          to the Death-Tree and be blindfolded;
shall once more hear the fatal sentence;
shall puff a last cigaret, request in calm
          the blindfold be removed;
shall toss off a witty aphorism; shall
          cast a cold eye on hat & sock;
shall hear the rifles be cocked and aimed;
shall hum a phrase from Ravel's Concerto; —
          and join the others
wherever they go wherever they go wherever they
          go.
Right Glove rises from the Banquet
unable; Right Glove sees, outside
bright eyes of the Cahoon; Right Glove
wonders at the silent faces, faces at the
candle-lit table and wonders and wonders
          and wonders which one . . .
as if no clock spoke, no hair grayed. But
Glove will stay, quiet, where you drop her;
Glove does not bother if another one appear.
Yet Glove is not an adjunct to anything;
her face is bright, and she is always where she is;
she is always where she is. Where she is, she is there.
But for a lost glove the firmament
creaks and breaks asunder;
O bow and then rise; O bow and then rise;
          O bow and then rise!)

Far afar an errand (in error) pronounces mitt's gauntlet.

Morpho frowns at a afar

(Morpho for moth)

The, And, If;

Resolved, Um Er, that that is that, Er.

(Parsecs)

…

O Steersman …

The taps And who asks If why Um is Um at all Er.
Eye's error and scope and extent and field of of focal disarray.

Focal array of feral display.

Feral display of (g)lovely black nesses in
a

congenial row array. Black winged bird (Wings

through the narrow place one life one …

Wyrdness of all termination and terminals and

Windy places, all

So far afar to her(e) it is it he measures. *Hwaet*

4 and 5 and 6 am.

∽

Soft buttery black leather fingers five.

Space digitally contrived and conspired a life. Quipu of a lost glove.

(Quipu: knotted-rope time measure string a)

Quipu as errand maker.

People walk past in bedazzled slow look, mid

Summer's dawn peeks through Um of thumb and a hollow of The and If and And;

Er as a reluctant volute, a tremble.
(Ears flared)

No one sees The.

Silence falls fast upon the dawn (but not for long)

. . .

Glove invisible, soft and leather and blackness in full
cognizance:

Never trust the human hand; it is A not
to be Er hinged to an unknown. Cahoon
and deceiver. Be Um. It is not A fit to
bear the Er, closest and cleave to. What
is the right Too to me, but a vague
semblance, as if This's and That's
old fallen tower and the moon. Old
bones mimicking a she who The Too [If *weeps*
is the right Too to me, but a vague
semblance, as if This's and That's
old fallen tower and the moon. Old

crow-faced mother who I was a very a very to the skin attached Too
to;

Thirteen hours uncounted, count them, left and right;

A radius of all my affections released

in perfect time, sequence and purest
sphere of affections. Sequence and purest
sphere of affections. To the skin attached
Too to a ah a radius of all my afflictions;

in perfect mathematic.

People big and near, and are then far and dear. Oldy and out of
range.

Use and function stop stopped with the fit is fled. When all ways
are:
Errand's errors.

In an Arrow's throw a throw away time a. Fingers of light are an
access to a dream of the who. Access to a a dream like an
empty glove. Useless solitary

[Er, thing:

thing hinged and a solitary A as if a world that cries herself up and
out. Ah yi! Utterance known to none. But like a footfall and
it is:

Jewel Beckett.

CHORUS 23 (*OLD* 16)

And what do I know of distance and Jewel Beckett?
Not a stitch of her is known to me;
Not a stitch of her is known to the moth;
Not a stitch of Jewel Beckett is known to a candle;
Not a stitch of Jewel Beckett is known to a myth,
    nor a meth, nor a moth, nor a muth;
Not a stitch of Jewel Beckett is known to Morpho,
    who is Morpho butterfly, who is Venus *Anadyomene*;
Not a stitch of Jewel Beckett is known to the Wood,
    nor to the mad in the Wood, nor to the squirrel in the
    Wood; nor to all the things of the Woods that are known to
    the Wood, and known to the Moon;
Not a stitch of Jewel Beckett is known to the City, to the
    walkways, the arcades, the fine gallerias;
Not a stitch of Jewel Beckett is known to the rest;
Not a stitch of Jewel Beckett: not her height, not her weight,
    not the meaning of her mysterious name;
Not a stitch of Jewel Beckett is a matter to bother;
Not a stitch of Jewel Beckett is a matter to care;
    not her ears, not her thumbs; not her hair
Not a stitch of Jewel Beckett is pictured anywhere;
Not a stitch of Jewel Beckett matters to the many;
Not a stitch of Jewel Beckett would cause any to stare:
What has she done?
What has she done?
She has picked with two fingers, up, from the ground
A lost left glove, and held it in the air.

∽

Scooped up!

What now world what now is set to tap out time?

Measure this: Awe ways woe won. *Hwaet*

Cahoon watches over And If and the emptiest of An. Five places, inside out and single hole in Time's Hollow. I'll not. Where is Lefty now? O Skin. Some moth and closets of a Spider and Math er Moth. Empty and filled up. Drat.

And and I forget And. Of course And. Drat.

The street the street the narrow place walkway arcade Galleria to a   a too extends as far as Jewel Beckett's

(perfection);

and her field of view. Wide and as narrow and we and it are:

(Um, too, Er)

∽

Far distant miles ago in an in (antiquity), Um, Er:

CHOIR TWENTY THREE & A HALF:

May Nazima Yamaha Nazimova be condemned,
to be removed, to the point furthest,
at the end of things, from the line AB, end points
of the Galleria or passageway in which the glove was left,
forming an isosceles triangle, at the end of space and time;
may she be condemned to hold forever her crumpled Right Glove
in a monkey jar with her left hand till the end of time.

She discovers her loss.

She discovers her gain.

Who at A wonder; is O is; what to do with and without; a single glove;

She imagines the estate of a lost glove, hopeless and alone.

WHY wonders Yamaha Nazimova;

WHY wonders Jewel Beckett;

Did I do what I do? Weird what I do: one glove and not two.

The Arcade and Galleria and narrow place and thin place glows dim a midsummer sunrise;

simple; as a glove goes:

As a glove with fingers of light; as a moth and as a spider;

in perfect mathematic.

All go apart, poles apart. Each a different radius of the sphere,
isotropically;

...

(Parsecs)

YAMAHA NAZIMOVA, gone to a far far place;

Farther than the domain of lost gloves YEA;
Farther than the moth and spider YEA;
Farther than the Mind of Morpho YEA;

CHORUS conclusus:

Resolved, that
a certain Jewel Beckett be crowned with a
          glove of gold and silver silk;
may her name be a byword among all the
          tribe of glove, especially the ones
lost in the world, hopeless, then found in a flash;

YEA YEA YEA.

May Nazima Yamaha Nazimova be condemned,
to be removed, to the point furthest,
at the end of things, from the line AB, end points
of the Galleria or passageway in which the glove was left,
forming an isosceles triangle, at the end of space and time;
may she be condemned to hold forever her crumpled Right Glove
in a monkey jar with her left hand till the end of time.

JEWEL BECKETT, has not gone she has not yet gone to a far
far place . . .
Yea she has not has not YEA,
The Left Glove lost now found is curled up, happily in a warm
spot, held in precious worth in her in her YEA

YEA YEA YEA precious Chinese rosewood drawer; in her secret
cabinet; in her apartment in the state/province of — ; in the
republic of — ; in the human heart YEA.

YEA YEA YEA.

Resolved, that that is that, Er;

The, and And, If too YEA.

And Um.

Moth and spider and also (YEA), and Morpho too (YEA YEA).

Far, far distant an Errand (perhaps one left too) pronounces the curse of unspeakable doing undoing upon the error in question, done in shame. Close by and closely an Errand (Yea!)
pronounces
ah an ah And and The and If and Um and Er in full stillness so that

Awe ways woe won. End is end now, for

Those that once made a noise in the world, now lie quiet …

(Reprise: *Whispered*

CHORUS seventeen:

Resolved, that:
We who know,
shall not know how;
shall not know how
to Inch and Foot;
shall not know end
from start and up
from where up goes
at the sheer drop
of an Inch at rest.

Resolved, that:
We who know,

shall not know how;
shall not know how
to Inch and Foot;
shall not know end
from start and up
from where up goes
at the sheer drop
of an Inch at rest.

This is the test that fingers five
obligate and make of it a
miracle: One two three four five.
What gloves the hand gloves the eye
and heart and soul and pins the
name of Inch to each as a mile's joy.
Resolve this; resolve that,
in the name of a Left Glove left behind.)

Awe ways woe won.

(Play is over now.)

MAC WELLMAN's recent work includes *The Difficulty of Crossing a Field* (with the composer David Lang) at Montclair State University in the fall of 2006, and *1965 UU* for the performer Paul Lazar, directed by Stephen Mellor at the Chocolate Factory in the fall of 2008. He is also working on two plays for chorus: *The Invention of Tragedy* (Classic Stage Company) and *Nine Days Falling* (commissioned by the Stuck Pigs Company of Melbourne, Australia). He has received numerous honors, including both NEA and Guggenheim Fellowships. In 2003, he received his third Obie Award, for Lifetime Achievement. In 2006, his third novel, *Q's Q*, was published by Green Integer, and in 2008 a volume of stories, *A Chronicle of the Madness of Small Worlds*, was published by Trip Street Press, and a new collection of plays, *The Difficulty of Crossing a Field*, was published by the University of Minnesota Press. His recent books of poetry are *Miniature* (2002) and *Strange Elegies* (2006), both from Roof Books. He is the Donald I. Fine Professor of Play Writing at Brooklyn College.